# MY
# GROWING
# YEARS

Translated from the original Bengali, *Chelebela*

SOMUDRANIL SARKAR

CLASSIX

**CLASSIX**

Published by **CLASSIX** (an imprint of Hawakal)

70 B/9 Amritpuri, East of Kailash, New Delhi 65
33/1/2 K B Sarani, Mall Road, Calcutta 80

Email info@hawakal.com
Website www.hawakal.com

Cover designed by Bitan Chakraborty

First edition (paperback) November 2022

Translation copyright © **CLASSIX** 2022

Typeset in Adobe Garamond Pro (12.5 pts.),
PTBN Arunima (13.5 pts.) & Trajan Pro (12 pts.)

Printed & bound in Thomson Press (India) Ltd.
New Delhi 110020



ISBN: 978-93-91431-18-1 (paperback)

Price: INR 300 | USD 14.99

*for*
**Sri Rudraprasad Sengupta**
for inducing courage to dream

# TO BE RECOGNIZED AS THE GENIUS

Somudranil makes this book his own.

You pick this book with the knowledge that anyone who reads the Bengali language, in all likelihood, would have read this iconic work in its original form.

As you begin reading *My Growing Years*, memories of the original come back—forgotten bits of incidents, anecdotes, and signature nuances of Tagore's inimitable storytelling.

And then magic happens. Very quickly, before you realize it, Somudranil deftly takes over and retells a tale that feels both intriguingly fresh and reassuringly familiar. I am amazed at how he finds that balance.

Some translators add their personal hues to the original material. Then there are those whose cautiousness not to have that extra coat makes the reading purely academic. Somudranil, I discovered, is of the rare kind who surrenders entirely to the emotional quotient of the material and lets his grasp on the language guide the rhythm of his prose. He is no more the Tagore who writes about his childhood. Instead, he becomes the younger

Tagore who lived those young years. That's where Somudranil makes this book his own.

*My Growing Years* paints a detailed picture of what it was like being Tagore when he was a kid. But importantly, it also astonishes you with the observational faculties of the little boy who grew up to be recognized as the genius he was.

As you read on, slowly and unknowingly, it will open up forgotten doors of memories of your own childhood. Images. People. Names. Incidents. Sounds. Smells. Moments. You will realize your childhood was as rich as Tagore's, with an ever-expanding understanding of life and its meanings. You'll feel you were once a little Tagore of your own childhood. That's what Tagore does to his readers.

And that's what Somudranil carries forward in his brilliant translation.

Sarthak Dasgupta
Filmmaker
November 2022
Mumbai

# TRANSLATOR'S NOTE

In Satyajit Ray's masterpiece *Agantuk* (*The Stranger*), the identity is beautifully questioned in the iconic frame when Sudhindra's barrister friend Prithwish Sengupta confronts that stranger, questioning where he had been over the last three-and-a-half decades. Utpal Dutt, who played the protagonist Manomohan Mitra, responded about how he learned about civilization and re-examined it. He claimed to have achieved more experience through meeting strangers from different corners of life. Identity mutates for what he believes.

Food for thought: Why did Satyajit Ray keep the English title of *Agantuk* as *The Stranger*? The Bengali title (*Agantuk*) translates into *The Unexpected/Unknown Visitor*. Perhaps, Ray delved into the narrative and developed macrocosmic countenance through microcosmic iteration. You can only understand my point when you watch the film from beginning to end.

Tagore was awed to note the stalling of identity concerning the ethos in which he resided, but he never defended on its behalf. The mutation is a part of progress, by augmentation of patterns, which helps to look forward to our possible promising future and doesn't wipe out the memory of the identity we've retained over the years. One can never forego their roots that define one's identity, culture, and values. Identity is an intrinsic feature that Tagore pens down in his second memoir, *My Growing Years*.

The signs and symbols of any language can appear otherworldly. Or perhaps, this is the common notion that people adhere to. By signs and symbols, I mean the cryptic appearance that might surface if thoughts are not well communicated. The translators should not make it any difficult for readers while reading a translated text. But it happens, nevertheless. Readers speculate that translated words would read difficult, as if it were a ground rule. They turn mountains out of molehills if faced with a challenge in decoding a sentence. The translation is the extraction of polyphonous aspects and churning it into a dialogue that might be unilateral or bilateral vis-à-vis open to interpretations. The seamless flow of thoughts should be retained. However, in the act of translation, one should not forget the identity of the source text.

Tagore's *My Growing Years* (originally, *Chelebela*) has been eye-opening. However, reading and re-reading the memoir raises a relevant question: Was this written for children? I doubt. Firstly, the text is regarded as his second memoir, and Tagore wrote this when he was almost eighty. So, in no way both language and experience can be accessible to children. I won't hesitate to confess that I had to read the memoir several times, especially between the lines, to decode specific meanings. For clarity, I'll cite a line or two from the Bengali original, followed by my translation:

> ক্রমে দিনের মরচে পড়া আলো মিলিয়ে আসে। শহরের পাঁচমিশালি ঝাঁপসা শব্দে স্বপ্নের সুর লাগায় ইট কাঠের দৈত্যটার দেহে।

> The light of the day fades away. The city would seize the paraphernalia of the waning cacophony, transpose that in some dreamy tune and paint it on the body of the demon city defined by brick and mortar.

The sentence: "The city would seize the paraphernalia of the waning cacophony, transpose that in some dreamy tune…," which young readers can hardly comprehend. Even the underlying thought wouldn't even reach them. However, my version is meant to make the pan-Indian readership more viable. My motive was to make it accessible to people who have no idea who Tagore is and what his achievements are. They know of him, like the rest poets, essayists, dramatists, lyricists, and so on. My target happens to be the people who, after picking up the book and scurrying through the pages, read a line or two—find it relatable—and take it back home. Relatability is a must factor that should not be ignored. I don't mean to offend any Tagore scholars, nor do I have the eligibility to discard the aesthetic quality the memoir carries. However, a spoken language's intonations, tone, and pitch embody much information about what the writer wants to convey. Therefore, to decode that, I had to hear the implied meaning behind the words. Hawakal has allowed me to do that, for which I am truly grateful.

I got a chance to read two English translations of *Chelebela* before I started working on this: *Boyhood Days* (Puffin Classics, with an introduction by Amartya Sen), translated by Radha Chakravarty, and *My Boyhood Days*, translated by Marjorie Sykes, published in the *Visva-Bharati Quarterly*. Both versions stand as exemplars in translated work.

While reading the subtext of the language and seeing through it, it is important to locate the intrinsic quality of the same. Let's take, for example, Argentinian filmmaker Gaspar Noé's *Vortex*, where he uses a technique known as split screen, where two different images are simultaneously at play. The movie shows an octogenarian couple who seems to gradually lose their memory. Also, this method demonstrates how the characters function even though they are almost out of sync and in different locations at the same time. The growing optimism to live in the moment makes it relevant in this setting. This goes hand in hand with the translation of *My Growing Years*. Throughout the text, Tagore cultivates nostalgia about the culture, the family he is proud to be a part of, the people he comes across while growing up, and the ethos. Every mortal thing fades into oblivion alongside the memory, which he documents. Tagore believes this will be documented in a way where it will make people dream and instill a belief that people have something to believe.

Now, going back to the memory part. Yes, how could I translate the essence of the memory that Tagore wanted to evoke:

> 1. I go on translating word-by-word, line-by-line.

> 2. Acknowledging the momentum, I have to comprehend the juncture that the original language generates, exudes, and thereby should present in such a way that will help it to move freely in the translated version.

I chose the latter. Translating the emotions of a culture needs extraction, and in that process, one cannot simply work as a google translator, making it superficial, redundant, and whatnot!

Kiriti Sengupta and Bitan Chakraborty have helped me substantially as I went ahead with translating *Chelebela*. I stumbled and staggered with the text; they stood by me and assisted me while I had difficulty reading between the lines. They rigorously prompted me to widen my horizon and look beyond the written lines. Almost akin to the beauty of Michelangelo's *The Creation of Adam*, where he aims to stretch toward the divine breath of life.

Somudranil Sarkar
October 2022
Calcutta

INTRODUCTION

Once Sri Nityanandabinod Goswami advised me to write something for children. A thought popped up—why don't I write about the boy Rabindranath? I tried to extract my experiences from the past. But it doesn't correspond to my present self. Back then, the lamp was guarded with smoke instead of emitting light. The young mind wasn't subjected to modern-day scrutiny. There was no line of demarcation between the possible and the impossible. I'm sure children would find the language accessible. The trance I was in faded into nothingness. I didn't let any change impede my tongue or the ethos concerning the time. But, this feeling itself surpassed childhood. I didn't allow this account to exceed the limits of my boyhood. In the end, the recollections arrived face-to-face with my teenage self. You will understand how a child's thought process evolves and accepts elements from diverse surroundings as you stand there. The whole point of calling the entire account my boyhood resonates with the growth and vitality of a kid.

The early stages of my life guided me to follow that path only. My boyhood reflects the ways the surrounding environment nurtured me in my childhood. As a minor, I accepted very little of the conventional method of education imparted to me. Some parts of this book can be found in *Jiban Smriti*, but it is as different as a fountain from a lake. *Jiban Smriti* is a story; this is a sweet-faint melody. That can be seen in a basket; this, in the tree. It is because the neighboring branches have embraced the fruits. It has been quite some time now that parts of my boyhood have found a place in a poetry book. It's called *Chorar Chobi* [*Picture of Rhymes*], which had rants by the naive and the mature. That resulted from my childish enthusiasm. In this book, my expression conforms to a prosaic form.

Rabindranath Tagore

**Notes:**

Sri Goswami came to Santiniketan in 1920 as a Research Scholar. Rabindranath asked Gosainji to teach Bengali and Sanskrit to the children of his school and this is what he did till the end of his service.

https://www.visvabharati.ac.in/NityanandabinodGoswami.html

*Jiban Smriti* also known as *My Reminiscences* was published by The Macmillan Company.

# 1

I was born in a time when it was called Calcutta and not Kolkata. Carriages would whoosh through the city, and dust shrouded the air. Whereas the horses were whipped repeatedly to move faster and faster. There were no trams, no buses, no cars. Work-Life wasn't very fast back then. Days would pass at a slow pace. On the way to the office, Babus would pull out the tobacco and smoke it, some in a palanquin and some in a shared car. The cars belonging to the rich folks were adorned with badges reinstating their aristocracy, whereas the hood of the cars was made of leather and remained half-veiled. In the Coach box, the coachman would sit with the turban tilted to one side of his head, two kinswomen at the back, fly whisk hung on their waists, and shout *heiyo* at the passers-by along the way.

By removing the curtains of the palanquin as soon as darkness descended, girls were allowed only to move in-out of the puffy darkness by removing the curtains of the palanquin. It was even considered shameful for girls to ride in the car. They didn't even use umbrellas to cover their heads, whether it be scorching heat or the rain. If a girl was found to wear chemise/shoes, then she'd be accused of copying a *Memsaheb*, and disgraceful elements would be hurled at them.

If a girl suddenly chanced to stumble upon a man, she would roll her veil over the tip of her nose and bite her tongue in shame. Soon after, she'd face her back at him. The doors remained shut because they couldn't step out of their houses. Similarly, they were restricted to travel by palanquins; the ones that belonged to the wives and maids of the upper class were covered with a thick yashmak carrying the bride-groom belonging to the upper class. There was another cover of thick linen cloth ornamented to denote the class. It looked like a moving grave. Porters would walk side by side with a brass-bound stick in their hand. Their job was to sit on the porch, rub their beards, and deliver money to the bank and the girls to their families. Once that was done, the porters would dip the palanquin with brides sitting inside it in the Ganges on the day of the festival.

Hawkers would come with many decorated boxes, and our porter Shiunandan would also want a share of the profit. Then there was the underpaid driver of the hired car, who would get into a heated argument in front of our door if dissatisfied with the tip. Our wrestler-sweeper, Sovaram, used to walk from left to right with a heavy knobstick. As he sat down to consume siddhi and sometimes raw radishes, we would scream *Radhakrishna'* to his ears. The more he laughed and beckoned to protest, the more stubborn we became. This was his trick to hear the name of the tutelary deity.

At that time, there was no gas or electricity in the city; we were taken aback when the kerosene light came into existence. In the evenings, a servant would come to the house and light the lamps powered by castor oil. This was also known as sej baati, which functioned when two wicks were ignited.

Our teacher would teach us the *First book* by Pyari Sarkar in that flickering light. First, we yawned, then felt sleepy, and finally rubbed our eyes. We were tired of hearing about Satin, our teacher's favorite, because of his academic nature. He'd rub tobacco powder in his eyes to avoid falling asleep. Oh wait, what about me? Well, there's no use talking about it. Nothing prevented me from falling asleep, not even the frightful thought of staying illiterate amongst all the other boys. As soon as the clock struck at 9:00 pm, my class would finally be over. I would rush to bed with tired eyes.

The path to the house from the courtyard was narrow, separated by a curtain, and a flickering chandelier would be seen suspended above. I used to walk, and my heart would quiver—God knows what is following me! A shiver would run down my spine. Ghost stories occupied people's minds. If a maid heard a *Shakchunni's* snuffle, she'd stumble down. It was a moody female ghost. Her mouth always watered as she thought about the fish. In the west corner of the house stood a thick-leafed almond tree. She would stand like a statue with one leg on a branch and the other on the cornice. Many people claimed to have noticed her presence. However, others refused to accept. When my brother's friend would laugh at these rumors, the servants thought that my brother's friend had no knowledge of theology, and the ghost would twist his neck one day to challenge his wisdom. The panic was palpable.

The water tap was not installed back then. In the month of *Magh-Fagun*, the palanquin bearer would bring water in pitchers from the Ganges—rows of pitchers remained filled with drinking water. They were kept in a dark room on the ground floor. God knows what creatures hid there in those damp rooms—as if their huge mouths were left wide open, eyes on their chests, ears on their heads, and legs inverted. I would feel a thud in my chest when I stepped into the

garden inside the house in front of that ghostly shadow. I wanted to run away. Due to the tides, water would come gushing through the roadside ditches. In my grandfather's time, the water from that drain was restricted to our pond. The water gushed out like a fountain when the doors were pulled down. The fish would want to show its swimming skill by darting in the opposite direction. In amazement, I would stare at the south porch. The pond was obliterated when garbage was dumped in it. Despite being a mirror to the green village for all these years, it soon disappeared.

Though the almond tree still stands there, the *Brahmadatyi* ceased to exist, despite having the advantage of standing with its legs stretched apart. The brightness has enhanced with time.


**Notes:**
Memsaheb: used while referring to any European woman.
Shakchunni: derived from the Sanskrit word Shankhachurni. In Bengal, the deceased soul of a married woman turns into a Shakchunni.
Brahmadatyis: are the ghosts of the Brahmins, who are regarded as patriarchal figures, dressed in the quintessential Bangali 'Dhuti'.
Siddhi: A kind of hemp popular in India
Magh and Falgun: Both the eleventh and twelfth months of the year respectively according to the Hindu Calendar.
*First Book*: Written by Pyari Charan Sarkar. The first English book made for native children.
Heiyo: A sound made by the palanquin bearers.

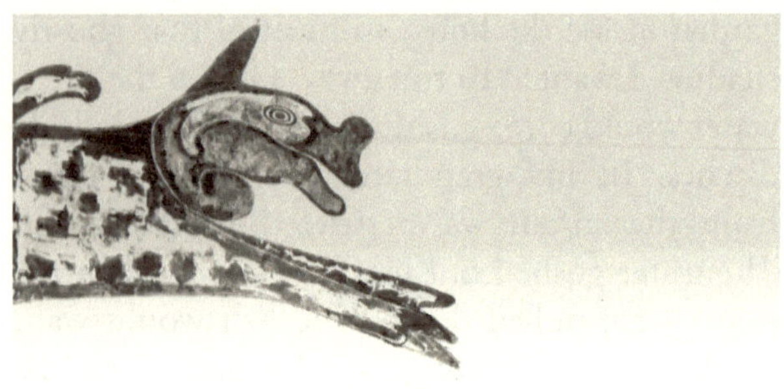

2

Palanquins were commonly used during my grandmother's time. They were spacious and royal. A palanquin would require eight bearers for each pole. The aristocracy faded with time like the sun-drenched clouds, and so did the gold bracelets, heavy earrings, and sleeveless red tunics worn by the bearers. In addition, colorful paintings on the body of the palanquin were all worn out. Also, coconut fibers came out from the seat. Despite becoming an antique piece of furniture, the palanquin found a place in the corner of our godown. At that time, I was about seven or eight years old and was not needed for domestic chores. That old palanquin was also discarded. This was precisely why it was so dear to me. It was like an island, and during my vacations, I would wear the guise of Robinson

Crusoe and play around the palanquin. Abandoning everything behind the closed door and bereft of surveillance—I felt completely safe.

Our house was never devoid of the crowd. Visitors would frequent every now and then. So be it any corner of the house I would be in, clamoring rendered by the servants was quite understandable. Pyari, the maid, would bolster a basket full of vegetables to the waist and enter the courtyard from the market. The water-bearer Dukhon would come with two pitchers filled with water and slung them to a shoulder pole. The weaver woman would enter the house with trending sarees and flaunt her trading skills. The goldsmith Dinu, who used to receive a monthly wage, would sit in a room beside the lane—he'd pull the hopper while following the house orders. Once finished with his work, Dinu would approach Kailash Mukherjee in the treasury room to ask for his outstanding payment. Mukherjee got a quill perched behind his ear. The carder would whip cotton from the old quits out in the yard. The blind wrestler would try a new technique with our porter Mukundaram. Thunderously the latter would slap his knee and do a few push-ups. There, a group of beggars would wait for alms.

The day would progress; the sun got scorching, and the alarm rung out on the porch.

However, the palanquin didn't follow the time. This was similar to what the Royal Court used to be in the ancient age. The King would go for his bath in the sandalwood water at the trumpet's sound (which served as an alarm) as the meeting ended. During holidays, my caretakers had their meals and fell asleep in the afternoon. I would sit alone. In my mind, the immobile palanquin would ply. Supported by the wind, the bearers thrived on my imagination. Sometimes, I would paint an imaginary road in my mind, traveling afar to different countries, which I made following the books I read. When the path led me to a dense forest, the sudden sight of a tiger's blazing eyes would send a shiver down my spine. Along with me, there would be Biswanath, the hunter, who would fire a shot and hush. There would be a deafening silence. And also, at times, my palanquin would transform into a *Mayurpankhi* and set sail in the ocean, but gradually it would disappear into thin air. I used oars to row the *Mayurpankhi*, and soon after, the water splashed, leading the waves to bulge. The sailor Abdul stood there at the tiller with a gnarled beard, shaved mustache, and bald head. And thus, my dream came to an end. Wait a minute, I knew him; he would bring hilsa fish and turtle eggs from the river *Padma*.

Abdul once told me a story. It was the end of the month when he had gone out fishing on his boat one fine day, and out of nowhere came *Kalboishakhi*. It was a terrible storm, and the boat was almost about to drown; just then, Abdul bit on the hawser rope, dived into the water, and managed to swim ashore. Reaching there, he held the rope vigorously and pulled up the boat. I wasn't delighted with the ending on a short note. On the contrary, I was bothered—why did the boat not drown, and how he survived? This didn't occur to me as a story at all. Repeatedly I asked, "What happened next?"

To this, Abdul replied, "Phew! I saw a panther with huge whiskers. During that storm, just on the other side of the ghat, the panther climbed up a *Pakur* tree to survive. The stormy wind uprooted the tree and went down into the river *Padma*. However, the tide set the panther afloat. It somehow managed to climb onto the bank I was in. I noticed the panther's ascent and made a noose out of the hawser rope. The beast, with its glaring eyes, drew near me. After swimming for long, its appetite had increased. On noticing me, its saliva dripped from its blood red tongue. Despite knowing people inside-out, the panther didn't know me. I called out, 'Here, boy' as it was about to leap, I darted the noose, and off it went and got hooked to its neck. The more the panther tried to free itself, the tighter the noose became. Eventually, that beast rolled out its tongue in the scuffle." I questioned again, "It didn't die, Abdul?"

"Die?" Abdul scoffs. "It wouldn't die so easily. Listen, there was a flood, but I had to return to Bahadurganj. So I harnessed the panther and made it drag the boat for about forty miles. I pricked it with my oar whenever it got grumpy, and off it went. You wouldn't believe how the panther covered the river that takes 10-15 hours to cross in about 1.5 hours. And don't ask me any further, dear boy; you won't get any answer." I said, "Okay fine, bunk the panther. Now tell me about the crocodile, will you?"

Abdul replied, "I have seen the crocodile's nose coming out of the water quite a few times. It lies down on the sloping river bank to bask in the sun. It flashes a horrendous smile. If I had a gun, I could have fought it. But alas, my license has expired. So allow me to narrate a funny incident."

"Once, there was this gypsy woman named Kanchi. After having tied her yeanling to a tree, she sat on the river bank and began sharpening a bamboo pole with the knife. Stealthily came the crocodile, and off it started dragging the yeanling by its leg down to the river. Having caught the sight, Kanchi jumped onto the crocodile's back and repeatedly started stabbing its neck with the sharpened bamboo pole. Finally, it unfastened its grip and plunged back into the water."

I was intrigued. I inquired, "What happened

next?"

Abdul answered, "Rest of the story got drowned in the river along with the crocodile. It will take time to fish that out. The next time we meet, I will put up a spy and tell him to query about it."

But Abdul didn't come. Maybe he had gone out to inquire.

This was my imaginative world inside the palanquin. Outside it, sometimes I would slip into the role of a teacher, and the railings of the verandah would become my students. In fear, they would all fall silent. Some of them were so naughty and had no interest in studies whatsoever. I threatened them that they would become illiterate if they did not study. My pupils wouldn't stop being naughty despite inflicting scars everywhere by repeated smacking. Stopping would put an end to my game as well. In addition, another game hosted a wooden lion. After having heard countless stories about the ritual of animal sacrifice, I decided to sacrifice my wooden lion. I tried smacking its back with a stick repeatedly. But then, I felt without a mantra, the ritual of sacrifice was incomplete, so I created my own mantra that read like this:

Chop chop roary lion head goes down
Die roary lion and become decrown
Pitter-patter walnut breaks woohoo
Plop slop inside does boohoo

All these words were borrowed, except walnut that belonged to me. I loved gobbling walnuts. 'Pitter-patter' would indicate the patting sound arising out of the stem, which was made of wood. And 'plop slop' would mean that the wooden tiger was not strong enough.

**Notes:**
Mayurpankhi: This is a peacock-shaped boat popular in Bengal, functioning as a major trope in folklore that didn't cease to exist or fade with time.
Padma: a major river in Bangladesh.
Kalboishakhi: In April-May, as the earth's surface is heated by intense sunlight, low-pressure centres are formed in Central and North-West India, and cool and high-pressure winds from the surrounding seas blow in that direction. As a result, storms and rains occur locally in the coastal areas of Orissa and West Bengal.
Pakur: Also known as the Indian bonsai tree belonging to the fig family.

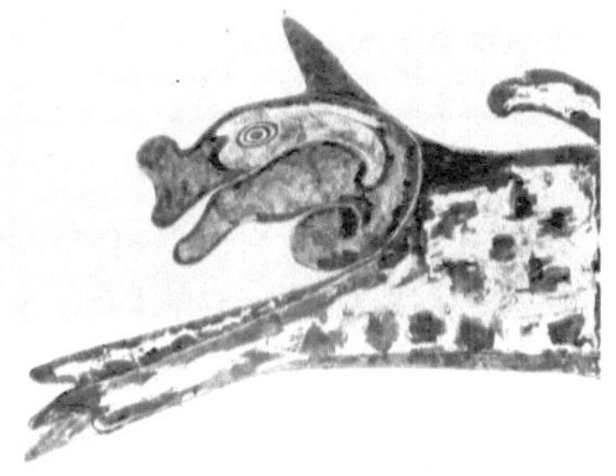

𝕵

It has been raining incessantly since yesterday evening. A flock of trees stands cluttered against each other. The birds are silent—they make me remember my childhood evenings. Back then, I'd spend time at the servant's quarter. The evenings were free of the rigmarole of learning English words and meanings. My older brother told me, "First, you should work on your Bengali basics and then learn English." So when all my fellow schoolmates started babbling things like I am up, he is down—I, on the other hand, had not even grasped the construct of BAD or MAD.

In the Nawabi language, the servant's quarter was referred to as *Tosha Khana*. We weren't aristocrats anymore; still, names such as *Tosha Khana, Daftar Khana* (Record Room), and *Baithaki Khana* (Drawing Room) were used in our household.

A castor oil lamp flickered on the southern side of our Tosha Khana, lighting the pictures of Ganesha, *Patachitra*, and Ma Kali. Somewhere near it, a lizard waited for its food—the insects. No furniture was there other than a worn-out carpet placed on the floor.

For your information, we behaved like the poor and didn't own any cars. We had a carriage and an old horse in a hut at a corner outside the courtyard, beneath a *Tetul* tree. We had simple dresses and began wearing socks quite late in our lives. So it was joyous when Brajeshwar went beyond his usual inventory and brought us bread and butter wrapped in a banana leaf. We were adapting ourselves to the decaying standards of high society.

The head servant, Brajeshwar, supervised our family gatherings. He had thick, curly hair alongside a salt and pepper beard. He had dry skin, was perpetually in a grave mood, and spoke harshly in a nibbled speech. After working under Lakshmimanta, his former boss (an influential man), his work-life became miserable. Brajeshwar ended up taking care of forsaken children like us. I had heard how he used to be a schoolmaster in a village school. He maintained the demeanor until the end of his life. Instead of saying, "The gentlemen are waiting," he would say, "It is to inform you that the gentlemen are waiting on the patio outside." And the head of our family would laugh at this. Brajeshwar was arrogant and obsessed with certain things in his life. To take a bath, he would walk down the pond and move the oily surface above the water with his hands for some time. After his bath, Brajeshwar would come out of the water and walk warily down the garden path. He'd wave his hands in a manner to keep away the unclean elements of the God-created world. That would otherwise stain his soul. He had strong opinions about proper and improper behavior. Though his words gained gravity because his neck was tilted to one side, he had a flawed supervisorship.

Brajeshwar was very greedy when it came to food. He did not serve us an equal amount. Less food for us would mean more for him. Whenever we sat down to eat, he would lift a *luchi*, wave it and ask softly, "Do you want more?" His tone would hint me to deny, and my 'no' pleased him. He would not insist on having the desserts as well. He had an immense craving for milk that I didn't have. There was a small cupboard in his room where he stored a big brass bowl full of milk, *luchi*, and curry in a wooden tray. Cats would stroll outside his window, helplessly smelling the food.

I never had a great appetite since my childhood. Though I ate little, it didn't make me any weaker than the boys who ate enough food.

My immunity system was exceedingly good, and I failed miserably despite my repeated efforts to escape the school. I tried different routes. Sometimes I'd dip my shoes in the water and walk around wearing them all day. Then I would lie down on the open roof in the month of autumn; despite getting soaked in sweat, there were no signs of coughing or wheezing. In times of indigestion, to use it as an excuse, I passed it off as a stomach ache.

However, in times of need, I would inform my mother about it. Hearing this, she would smile deep inside but did not show a sign of doubt. Instead, she would call the servant and tell him, "Go and inform the tutor that he can take a leave today."

Our old-fashioned mothers used to think it wouldn't harm the children if they missed a class or two. But the present day mothers wouldn't leave us with an option but to attend the tuition and some complimentary smacking alongside it. Maybe, with a smirk, they would have also made us drink castor oil. If I ever had a fever, nobody bothered about it but passed it as a slight rise in the temperature.

Doctor Neelmadhab would come to my rescue. I had no clue about the thermometer as he did not use it. He would examine me and prescribe medications like castor oil. He would also ask me to eat less and drink boiled water in small quantities. I was allowed to have cardamom. After three days of my adhering to these instructions, I was allowed to have *Mourala* curry with steamed rice. It was no less than a heavenly feeling.

I do not recall if I ever had a fever. Malaria was alien to me. I do not remember what quinine is. But I remember how castor oil qualified as the king of medicine. I never had any scar on my skin. And to this date, I have no idea what measles or chickenpox is. I felt obstinately healthy. If mothers want their children to remain healthy, I would advise them to hire a servant like Brajeshwar, who would save on the expenses of food and doctor. Especially in times of inflation of mill flour and adulterated ghee oil. One must know that, back then, chocolate had not yet been made available in the market. There was a pinkish candy made with molasses available for one paisa. They were very sticky, and once you kept them in your pockets, you would feel uneasy. I don't think the boys of today's age have any knowledge about such candies. It was strange how these sugar-coated candies ceased to exist. What happened to those fried spices that were available in cone-shaped packets? What happened to the sesame *gojas*? Are they still available? If not, there is no need to bring them back.

I would spend the evenings listening to

Brajeshwar as he recited the seven cantos of Krittibas's Ramayana. Kishori Chatterjee would drop by at times while Brajeshwar went on reading. The former knew the Ramayana *Panchali* and its tune by heart. All of a sudden, Kishori Chatterjee would take over the front seat, overthrow Krittibas, and begin his version of the *Panchali* with an overwhelming fervor—

*Hear me, O Lakshman*
*Inauspicious thundering here and there*
*Danger danger everywhere*

With a smile on his face and a sparkling bald head, melodies of the rhymes jingled as they streamed out his throat. The verses rendered a sound, as did the river water when it plodded against the pebbles underneath. He would move his hands and feet to express himself. One thing Kishori Chatterjee regretted the most was Dadabhai's (as he called me) non-participation in the *Panchali* troupe. I failed to get into it because of my voice. Had I joined, I would have made a mark in my country. As the night descended, our session would come to an end. The fear of ghosts would send a shiver down my spine, and hurriedly I would rush off to my mother's room. She would play cards with her aunt at that time. The decorated Parquet floor shone like Ivory with a blanket that would be

put out on the divan. At times I would make such a fuss that my mother would throw up her cards and say, "If  he continues to bother us, auntie, please go and tell him stories."

After washing our feet on the verandah, we would drag grandma to the bed. Then would begin the magical story of the princess who had been asleep for ages in the demon city. But, I would think, even if the princess woke up,  who would awake me? Then, as midnight approached, the jackals would begin their habitual howling. Back then, the old houses in Calcutta appeared haunted by their wail.

**Notes:**

Luchi: Having its origin in the Bengal region, it is made with Maida flour in a round shape and is deep-fried.

Mourala: Hailing from East Bengal these are small fishes normally eaten after deep-fried with mustard paste.

Goja: This is a quintessential sweet popular in Bengal where the dough of pastry is layered, shredded, deep-fried and dipped in syrup.

Panchali: In Assam and in Bengal Panchali is a kind of ballad vis-à-vis an oral narrative form.

Patachitra: A scroll-based painting, popular in West Bengal and Orissa.

Tetul: Also, known as the tamarind tree.

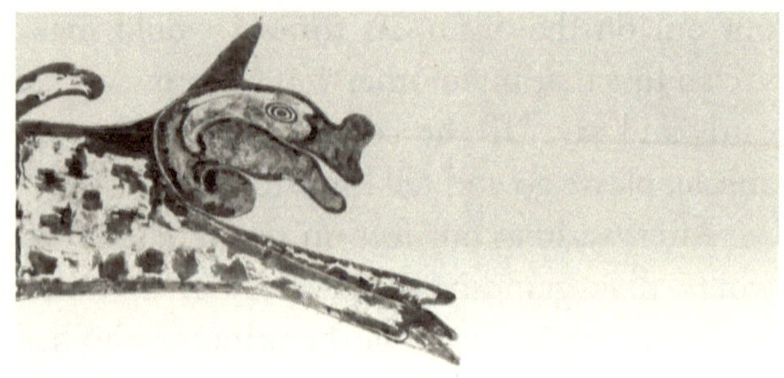

# 4

While we were young, the evenings in Calcutta were timid, unlike today. Nowadays, as the sun sets, approaching darkness dissipates with the electric light. At that time, the city dwellers didn't rest. Although finding a job was challenging like the wooden blocks that were burnt in the oven, the coal continued to hold fire in its core. The boisterous ethos got replaced by the mundane life. The oil mills were off for the evening, the steamer's whistle was silent, the workers left the factories, and the buffalo-drawn carts moved to the tin-roofed city stables. The city that was fiercely functional at day time began to throb slowly. Buying and selling at the roadside stalls remained the same, but the enthusiasm receded. Several cars and other vehicles were plying in the city with a relaxed rhythm.

As the day ended, all unfinished work escaped to a blanket of the night sky. The evening sky hung mysteriously, both on the inside and outside. While returning from Eden Gardens, the grooms would yell in joy out on a ride by coachmen. In *Chaitra-Baishakh*, the peddlers would go around screaming, "i-ice." They carried large pots filled with salty iced water. Inside it remained small tin cones containing Kulfi (well, that's what we called it), now known as ice cream. Stranded in the verandah, staring at the street, I got excited whenever I heard a peddler screaming ice. Then there would be peddlers selling Bela flowers.

The gardeners, who dangled around with their springtime flower baskets, have ceased to exist. The fragrance of Bela garlands that the women wore on their hair buns filled the air. Before taking a bath, the women would sit at their doorstep with a hand mirror and tie their hair in braids. They would make braided hair buns in different styles.

They wore black *Forasdanga* sarees that were folded and pleated before use vis-à-vis the fashion of the bygone days. The barber's wife would come to scrub their feet with a pumice stone and then paint them in *alta*. Women like her were the gossipers.

Earlier, while returning home from college and office, people refrained from standing on the tram's footboard as they were in no rush to reach the football field. Nor did they make a crowd in front of the cinema halls. There was a growing interest in theatre plays. But alas, I was only a child then. At that time, the boys were not allowed the pleasure enjoyed by the adults, even from a distance. But as we gathered courage, we were told, "Shoo off and play."

Even when we played clamorously, we were directed to keep quiet. But when the grown-ups celebrated something, far from being silent, they'd sound even more like a fizzy fountain hurled at us. Leaning on the verandah railing, I would stare at how the ballroom got bright as soon as the evening descended. One after the other, big coaches would arrive by the porch. Our elder brothers would escort the guests upstairs, greet them with a rose bouquet and sprinkle rose water from the *gulaab paash*. This was a ritual. Then they watched a play, but I had never been able to decode one thing: Why did that high-caste heroine sob?

I had a great deal of curiosity to know about that entire concept. Though I understood that the woman who sobbed was from a high caste, it was my brother-in-law in disguise. In those times, male and female family members had a boundary between them (separated by a curtain), and so did the adults and the children.

The singing and dancing would waltz to the

dazzling chandeliers in the living room. Men smoked hookah while the women sat behind the lattice-screened windows in the dim light with betel boxes. There, other female guests would gather and gossip about domestic chores. However, kids would be shooed off to bed by that time. Our servants Piyari or Shankari would read out stories that came drifting to our ears—

In the moonlight, the flower blooms…

Notes:

Foras Danga: Chandannagar, a city in West Bengal was earlier known as Foras Danga which literally translates into French land.

Alta: A red dye produced from lac, is normally used in Bengali, especially in times of ceremonies and festivals, where women are adorned with the said thing.

Paan: Consists of betel leaf containing nut, lime, raisins, cardamom, red-katha pastes. The leaf is wrapped up and chilled before it is served.

Chaitra and Baisakh: The first and second months in the Hindu calendar.

Gulaab Paash: Rosewater sprinkler.

# 5

Previously, a few wealthy householders practiced amateur *Jatra*. It was imperative to recruit boys with a shrill voice. One of my uncles led an amateur troupe. He was a talented playwright. And happily helped the boys with the performance. As wealthy families loved amateur *Jatras*, professional *Jatra* was equally popular all over Bengal. *Jatra* troupes formed overnight in every neighborhood by some well-known and influential people. The founders weren't necessarily of some high caste or highly educated but became the leaders of those groups because of their merit. Our house would host *Jatra* performances once in a while. But as a child, I wasn't allowed to watch *Jatra*. Nevertheless, I managed to look at the rehearsals. Troupe members would gather in the verandah and smoke. The aroma of tobacco lifted the air. The members had dark circles and long hair and behaved like adults despite being pretty young. Their lips were stained by chewing *paan*. They kept all the makeup tools inside a tin box. As it was an open entrance to the courtyard, the audience would arrive in numbers. This gave rise to the surging chaos that spread to the lane beyond and across Chitpur.

As the clock struck nine in the evening, Shyam held me in his fist as a hawk pounced on a dove and said, "Your mother's calling you; time to go to bed." To avoid being humiliated by getting dragged, I would accept my defeat and hurry back to the bedroom. A clamor would arise outside my room, and the chandeliers would glare up, but the inside remained peaceful. The brass lamp flickered on its stand. However, deep in my sleep, I could feel people dance with the *Sam* as it initiated rhythm on the tabla.

Quite religiously, the adults forbade us from everything. But God knows why they went soft in their heart and allowed the children to attend the *Jatra* performances. The performance was based on the legend of Nal and Daymanti. Before it began, I slept like a rock until 11 pm. Repeatedly we were told that they would wake us up just before the show. I knew the precepts of the elders, so I didn't trust them. But, since they were old and we were young, they naturally acted as they pleased.

That night, I managed to get up from bed. I did this because my mother promised to wake me. Also, there was another reason that I needed some extra effort to stay awake after 9 pm. I woke up, dragged myself out, and was completely startled. Light shone brightly from the chandeliers on the ground and the floor above it while it swaddled the courtyard like a white sheet—it appeared bigger than usual.

On one side, we would have senior members of our family and our guests, while on the other, uninvited people would join and crowd the space. The audience would comprise eminent people—some wore gold chains that hung down their bellies. They came in good numbers alongside the rich and poor, who huddled together to watch the *Jatra*. Most of the people in the audience would be "the lowest of the low," which was what the respected gentlemen called them.

The musical dialogues were written by people who used reed pens but never learned English. Melodies, dance, and stories were all collected from rural setups—teachers didn't polish the same. When we came to watch the performance with our elder brothers, we were given some coins in a folded handkerchief. It was a ritual to throw the hanky with the money inside it at the exact moment, as a cheer. This was extra earning for the troupe, and the host would reach a good reputation.

Though the night came to an end, the *Jatra* didn't. I didn't know who took me to my mother's room as I would fall asleep. Even if I knew that it'd be no less than an embarrassment for a little boy who sat confidently amongst the elders and threw money at the performers. It's late morning with the blazing sun in the sky as I would wake up. The sun had risen and I hadn't, never happened even once.

Nowadays, in the city, entertainment flows without any interruption. A film would be randomly screened, and people could watch the show with affordable tickets. In those days, *Jatra* seemed like digging the sand for water in the dry river bed at long distances. *Jatra* would last for a few hours; visitors would stop by and quench their thirst.

The old times were like the prince who disbursed alms to the needy in and around his area. The present-day is like the traders' son, displaying glittering commodities at the crossroads, thereby attracting customers from the lanes and bylanes.

**Notes:**
Jatra: A folk-theatre form from Odisha, which became widely popular all over Bengal.
Sam: The first beat concerning the tal, relevant in terms of tabla.

Brajeshwar was the head servant. Shyam, who was from Jessore, was the second in command. He was the typical rural countryman whose dialect was unlike the Calcuttans. He would say *tenara* and *onara* instead of *tara* and *ora* (them and they), *jati hobe* and *khati hobe* instead of *jete hobe* and *khete hobe* (must go and eat). Brajeshwar would affectionately call me 'Domani.' He was dark-skinned, had big eyes, hair soaked in oil, a strong and well-built body, and was devoid of complexities. His nature was not harsh, and he was very kind to children. He would tell us numerous stories of dacoits. As the fear of ghosts permeated people's minds, the reports of robbery lingered in every household. Not that it reduced, since murders, injuries, and plundering continue to occur. Police wouldn't catch the real culprits—nothing is interesting in these because it's all news. Earlier, anecdotes of bandits were weaved into stories and passed on for ages.

During our childhood, many people were found to be members of some dacoit gangs in their heydey. Among them were big-shot *lathials*, and many young guns aspired to learn the art of *lathi khela* from the masters. People would salute them whenever they heard the names of such masters. Robberies were unlike violent murders. It meant the synthesis of courage and greatness of the heart. Alongside this, the gentlemen clan set up training schools at their homes to promote the skill of *lathi khela*. Prominent *lathials* were looked up to by the dacoits, who avoided entering the territory of the *lathials*. Many zamindars made robbery their primary business. I heard a story once about a dacoit who hid his gang at the river Delta. On the no-moon night during the puja, the gang returned to the Kali temple with a severed head as a sign of religious sacrifice before Mother Kankali to honor the goddess. On seeing this, the zamindar slapped his forehead himself and screamed, "Oh God! What have you done! This is my son-in-law!"

Tales of Raghu and Bishu dacoits were the talk of the day. They were completely righteous in their actions since they'd notify their victim before attacking and never struck dishonorably. People froze in fear whenever they heard the cry of these dacoits from afar. It was forbidden in their custom to lay hands on women. Once a girl, disguised as Kali, took advantage of the situation and lifted the saber blade to rob the dacoits.

A display of dacoit skills was organized at our house. They were young men, well-built, and had long hair. After tying a piece of cloth on a big wooden pestle, clutching the piece of cloth between their teeth, they would toss it over their shoulder and catch it flawlessly. One held a man by his shaggy hair and swung him around. Then some would use the staves to jump and land themselves on the first floor. Almost flew like a bird through the opening between a person's outstretched hands.

They also exhibited how they slept peacefully at night after carrying out the robbery some 10-15 kilometers away. They would plant half-bent wooden pieces on the long poles for resting their feet. These crutches were known as Ran-pa. Holding the tip of those poles and resting the feet on the attached wooden piece, one step would equal 10 steps if done in standard steps while walking. With this, a man ran faster than a horse. Although I didn't intend to commit robbery, I once tried to induce this habit of walking on poles amongst the boys in Santiniketan. I would place my hand over my beating heart and think how much I romanticized the robbery coup, connecting them with tales that Shyam had told me.

On a Saturday night, when crickets chirped from the bushes in the southern garden, we were told the story of the dacoit Raghu. My heart pounded amidst the flickering light in the dark room. The next day was a holiday, and I chanced to board the palanquin. It began to move without any push or effort to an unknown destination. While the hint of danger inculcated from last night's story still lurked in my mind, I was apprehensive but excited to enjoy the thrill.

In silence, the pulse of the darkness thumped with the rhythm of the palanquin bearers—Hayi, Hui, Hayi, Hui. The dreading trepidation threw me into a jiffy. On the vast plain, the air trembled intensely; somewhere out there shimmered the sparkling sand close to the darkened lake. The crooked *Pakur* tree with its unfurled branches bent over the splintered ghat.

The horror of the stories amassed underneath the trees of that unknown field. The closer we advanced, my heartbeat was faster. Over the coppice appeared the tips of several bamboo trees. The palanquin bearers would stop there to change shoulders at that point. They drank water, relaxed, and tied wet towels around their heads. And what next?

The dacoits would give out a loud cry:

*"Re re re re re re!"*

**Notes:**

Lathial: A social group in rural Bengal who are known to practice the martial art form known as lathikhela.

Pakur: A tree from Fig family.

Lathi khela: Bengali martial art form that involves combat with sticks.

7

From morning to night, our home-based education system continuously produced its cacophonous sound. The third of my elder brothers, Hemendranath, strict in his nature, looked after the operations. If the tanpura strings are tuned too tightly, they might break. Similarly, the plethora of knowledge he dumped on us sank like the freight on a shallop that flipped eventually. My knowledge was at a loss.

Hemendranath began educating his elder daughter, Pratibha. She was eventually admitted to Loreto Convent School. Before that, Pratibha had adeptly mastered the basics of the Bengali language. She was also trained in Western music, although it didn't stop her from learning Indian music—no member of the noble families could match her excellence. One major advantage of western music is its composition and how it adheres to the scales with sheer authenticity. Playing piano does not mean any rift in the rhythm, and the ears get acquainted with the melody.

As a child, Pratibha took her lessons in Eastern classical music from Vishnu. I, too, was made to train under him. Nowadays, any famous or less-popular Ustad would scoff at the songs Vishnu had selected for our training. These were at the lowest level when it came to matching rhyming standards. Let me give you one or two examples—

> *There was once a gypsy girl*
> *In our neighborhood, she dangled*
> *Charmed us with her art*
> *And won our heart*

> *What magic were they—*
> *Oh, grandma,*
> *In tattoo's sting, I've cried ah*
> *Oh, grandma!*

I also remember a few lines in bits and pieces:

> *Sun and moon have bowed to defeat*
> *Firefly torch lamp, marking age*
> *Moghul-Pathans withdraw clans*
> *Weaver reads the Farsi language*

*Oh, Ganesha's mother,*
*Irritate Kolabou no more*
*If its flower blooms and blossoms*
*You won't know how many children she'll bear*
One may recall lines that ooze the aroma of past, forgotten news:

*Once there was a bush of poppy*
*Meant for dogs alone*
*Carved he there his throne*

Nowadays, practicing Sa Re Ga Ma Pa on the harmonium is essential. And only after that a light Hindi song is taught. Earlier, people who educated us felt that childhood had its kindred needs. Therefore, children were more prone to learning simple Bengali words than Hindi. Also, the indigenous rhythms didn't care about the Hindustani *bol* of the tabla and the *bayan*. It danced itself into our pulses. Children were introduced to literature through nursery rhymes recited by their mothers and experimented further by weaving music to those verses. We were taught music the same way and were the first to go into trials for such experiments. Harmonium had not yet stepped in to wipe out the trace of our regional music. Resting the tanpura on my shoulder, I practiced my lessons and did not enslave myself to the western pursuit by pressing the piano keys mechanically. My only weakness was that I couldn't continue learning anything for a long time. I filled my bag with whatever I came across, pleasurably picking things along the way. Had I learned anything by heart, the Ustad nowadays wouldn't even dare trivialize me. Well, I have had plenty of opportunities. As long as Hemendranath taught us, I babbled Brahma Sangeet before Vishnu. Whenever I felt the urge to learn a new tune, I would stand in the doorway and pick up whatever I heard.

Hemendranath practiced Oti Gojogaminire in Behag raga and I, standing behind the door, picked up the tune. It was easy to surprise my mother when I sang that same tune in the evening.

Our family friend Srikantababu would go on singing all day long. He sat on the verandah and rubbed jasmine oil on his body before his bath. He held the hookah in his hand, and the smell of amber-scented tobacco filled the air. And his humming sent the boys into a trance and drew them close to him. He didn't teach us any songs but sang them to us, and we would pick up the tune without our knowledge. When he could not hold back his excitement, he would stand up, play the sitar, and dance to its rhythm. With a grin, his big eyes would sparkle in joy. He would sing—Mai choro Braj ki Basuri and wouldn't stop until I joined him.

Previously, keeping the house door open to

everyone was deemed congenial. There was no curiosity to know a person before welcoming them. If anybody dropped by without prior notice, not only were they well-received, but they were also offered food to eat and a bed to rest in.

Once, an unknown guest arrived at our home, who brought his tanpura wrapped in a quilt held to his hip. He opened his bundle of belongings, stretched his legs, and sat down in a corner of the living room. Kanai was in charge of providing hookah, so he offered the same to the stranger.

Alongside tobacco, *paan* was served to the guests as well. The morning chore for the women was to stack up the *paans* in piles out in the reception room. Quickly they would apply lime paste on the *paan*, stuff it with masala, and fold and secure it with a clove on the back. Then, they would stack it up in a steel bucket and cover it with a moist cloth. In the room beneath the staircase, the demand for preparing tobacco would be on the rise. Ash-clad roasted tobacco was stuffed inside a big earthen pot. While the hookah pipes hung like snakes, the coils had a rose water fragrance. Before the people even took the stairs, they were greeted by the scent of amburi tobacco. At that time, everyone was held equal in the household. That *paan*-stacked bucket has vanished with time. The hookah servers have abandoned their clothes. They now work at the sweetmeat shops and knead the dough of three-day-old *sandesh*.

The unknown guest stayed back for a few more days. Nobody questioned his intention. In the morning, I would pull him out of the mosquito net and make him sing. People who are not in the habit of learning rules get accustomed to irregular education. He would sing his morning tune: Bangshi Hamari Re.

As I grew up, a music teacher named Jaduvatta came to stay in our house. However, he committed a grave mistake of harboring the desire to teach me music. But alas! He failed to do so. I had picked up a few things secretly. I grew fond of the song Rum Jhum Barkhe Aju Badarwa in Kafi raga; it stayed back to this day. Even now, when I compose my rain songs, I keep sprinkling a note or two from that song.

A new trouble surfaced when a guest arrived at our house without prior notice. He had earned quite a reputation as a hunter preying on tigers, although it seemed too strange for a Bengali. This is why I stayed glued to his room. We were astonished to hear how he fell into the tiger's clutches and didn't get bitten in any way. Perhaps he forged his own story by getting inspired by the wide-open jaws of the tiger as he had seen in the museum. This didn't cross my mind then, but now I can perceive it clearly.

He made that up. Back in that time, I was busy supplying *paan* and tobacco for such a heroic figure. The alaap of Kanhra raga would faintly reach my ears, even from a distance.

This was my chapter on music. Hemendranath diligently tried his best to strengthen the foundations for other branches of studies as well. However, nothing fruitful came out of it because of my nature. I guess Ramprasad Sen had someone like me in his mind when he wrote, "O heart, you do not understand the art of cultivation."

I never cultivated anything on any given day. Having said that, let me tell you of some fields of education that got plowed.

I would get out of bed early in the morning to practice wrestling. In winter, my whole body would shiver. We were trained by a popular wrestler in the city who went by the name of Kana Palowan. On the northern side of the hall, there was an empty land known as *Golabari*. The name that survived suggested that all of rural life had not yet been washed out by the city life, some of that rustic life still thrived. At the beginning of urban civilization, the *golabari* would be stacked with a stock of grains for an entire year. The sharecroppers on our territory would carry a portion of grains to our doorstep. At the end of this *golabari* wall stood the wrestler's space. To create it, a ground was dug and loosened to a foot and a half, and a considerable amount of mustard oil was poured into it. It was merely child's play for the wrestler to pin me down. After getting smeared in the soil, I would put back my t-shirt, and take my leave. My mother did not appreciate me going out in the mornings to return with a dust-smeared body. Fearing that her son's skin might get darkened and blemished; she would, during the holidays, put full effort into scrubbing me. Fashionable housewives of today's age buy all the skincare materials from shops that sell foreign merchandise. But in those times, housewives made ointments with their own hands. It consisted of almond paste, orange peels, and so on. Had I known and remembered the ingredients, I could've set up a shop and sold it under the name of Begumbilash. Making a profit similar to that of a *Sandesh* store.

On Sunday mornings, I sat on the verandah and underwent scrubbing. The mind would grow restless to skip that. Incidentally, a rumor drifted amongst the school boys that whenever a child takes birth in our house, he or she got bathed in wine, which is why their complexion appears like that of the Europeans.

After returning from the wrestling arena, a student from medical college would come to teach me the art of identifying human bones. A skeleton hung on the wall of our room, and at night the bones would swing and make a rattling sound. After dealing with the bones, though it was a difficult process, I wasn't afraid of skeletons anymore.

As soon as the clock on the porch struck 7 am, Nilkamal master would arrive, as he couldn't afford to waste even a minute. He was thin, but his health was like his students—never failed. Not even for once did he have a headache or something. As a result, we lost our chance of skipping our lessons. I would bring my slate and books to the table, and he would draw mathematical figures on the blackboard with chalk in Bengali—arithmetic, algebra, and geometry. In literature from Sita's Banabas, I would jump onto Michael Madusudan Dutt's Meghnadh Badh Kabya. Alongside these, I was taught natural science as well. My teacher Sitanath Dutta would drop by at times and bring along the latest scientific news, which I had only heard faintly. But with his arrival, the news got verified. Once Heramba Tattvaratna, the Sanskrit scholar, came and began teaching *Mugdhobodh* (the Sanskrit grammar), which I learned by heart without understanding a word of it. In this way, the more and more pressure I felt through reading all morning, yet my mind would seek an escape to discard those burdens. All my memorized knowledge wanted to escape by carving a hole in the net of mugged-up knowledge. And, this stopped Nilkamal master from boasting about his student's intellect.

On one side of the verandah sat old Niyamat, who wore thick-lensed spectacles that hung down his nose. He leaned down, sewed clothes, and took breaks occasionally for his routine namaz. I would stare at him and think how lucky this Niyamat fellow must be. When my mind got exhausted while solving the sums, I would hide my eyes with the slate and look down from beneath it at the front porch; Chandrabhan would stand there and comb his long hair with a kankoi (a thick-wooden comb). He would pleat them in two parts and tuck the ends behind his ears. The young guy who sat next to him wore a bracelet called a kankon, was a thin guard, and smoked tobacco. The horse standing there at the same place had already gobbled up its allotted hay from the bucket. While the crows jumped and pecked at the scattered lentils. Noticing that our dog Johnny's sense of duty gets charged up, he barks and shoos them away. I had planted a few custard apple seeds in a dust heap at a corner of the verandah. My mind just fidgets as it grows curious to see the young leaves sprout. The moment Nilkamal left, I would rush to see the seeds and water them. Eventually, my expectations turned oblivious as the broomstick brushed off the residue away, the same thing that was plied to create the heap.

As the sun rises it engulfs half of the courtyard

in shadow. It's 9 am. The short, dark-skinned Gobinda would hang a dirty yellow towel on his shoulder and take me for a bath. At 9:30 am, a daily portion of rice, dal, and fish curry would be served routinely. I didn't like to eat all of that.

At 10 am came hurtling the mirthless cries of the mango sellers peddling unripe mangoes. The clangour ousting of the brass utensils of the hawker would linger even when they moved further away.

At the corner lane on the house roof, the elder wife would be found drying her hair in the sunlight. Her two daughters were busy playing with shells and were in no hurry. Since it wasn't mandatory those days for girls to be at school on time. How I wished; had I been born a girl, my life would have been more joyous. But alas! The old horse dragged me in the palanquin to my isolated Andaman, where I remained exiled from 10 am to 4 pm. I would return home from school after half-past four. The gymnastics master would come at that time. He would make me exercise and balance my body on a wooden pole for an hour. As soon as he left, the drawing teacher would arrive.

The light of the day fades away. The city would seize the paraphernalia of the waning cacophony, transpose that in some dreamy tune and paint it on the body of the demon city defined by brick and mortar.

An oil lamp burns in the reading room. Aghor master arrives and starts teaching English.

*The Reader* as the book was called, with its dark cover, waited to swoop on me. The book cover was loose, and the pages were stained and torn. I wrote my name in English all over the places, in capital letters. I would often feel drowsy, and  when it happened, with a wrench, I would wake myself up. I spent significantly more time not reading than I did studying.

When I finally threw myself into the bed, I found my moments of respite. I would listen to stories that never reached their end:

"The prince has embarked on a journey to an endless terrain..."

**Notes:**

Choon: Catechu, a kind of herb extracted from betel leaves, and applied to paan.

Naglok: In Hindu mythology, naglok refers to the residing place underground for snakes beneath the earth.

Bol: The rhythm pattern in North Indian Classical music is known as bol.

Sandesh: A kind of dessert having its roots in Bengal is made with milk and sugar.

Golabari: Storehouse.

Bayan: The bigger drum in Tabla.

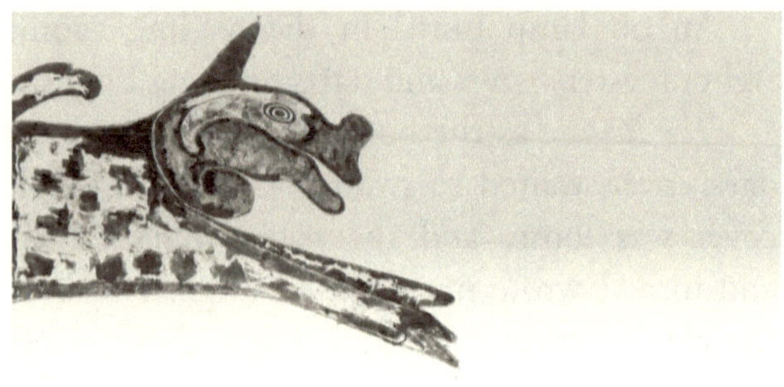

I can perceive the difference between then and now whenever I see the roofs of modern houses uninhabited by ghosts or humans. I told you before, dearest *Brahmadatyi* failed to accept open-mindedness and fled. The rumor about the ghost resting his foot on our terrace's cornice no longer exists. Now, the crows squabble through the mango seeds there. Under the roof, humans remain confined to the four walls that look like a carton.

I remember the enclosed terrace, where my mother sat on the mat and gossiped with her companions. They did not discuss anything authentic or constructive per se, but they only wanted to pass their time. In those days, there was no standard stock of valuable interests to fill the hours of the day. The day was not like finely woven cloth but a net full of holes. The tattles were light and trivial, whether they were social events for males or ladies. Braj Acharjee's sister, who was known as Acharjini, was the most important person among my mother's companions. She was in charge of offering daily updates at those meetings. She'd often bring in some strange or scary news or would instead make them up, leading the ladies to delve into expensive rituals for forestalling the impending calamity and, thus, ensuring domestic concordance.

In the meetings, I would often flaunt my textbook knowledge, telling them that the sun stretched at a distance of 9 crores of miles from the earth. From the second part of the *Riju Path,* I recited the Sanskrit verses from the Valmiki's Ramayana in bits and pieces. Ma wasn't curious about my pronunciation, but she was surprised to hear me recite and thought my wisdom outran that 9 crores of miles. None would have thought of listening to these shlokas from anybody else but the sage *Narada*.

The terrace remained occupied by the women for a long time. It was connected to the pantry. The lemons kept out on the terrace in the sunlight were eventually made ready for the pickles. The women would sit there with their brass bowls filled with Kalai and paste it. While drying their hair, they would make lentil dumplings. The maids would spread out the washed clothes on the roof wire for drying. The dhobi's work was relatively easy back then. Raw mangoes were sliced and would be left to dry to make amshi. The mango juice was poured into molds, layer after layer. These molds were made of black stones and came in various shapes and sizes. The jackfruit would be marinated in mustard oil and kept out in the sunlight for seasoning. Catechu was created very carefully, and I remember it vividly for a reason. When my school teacher told me he had heard about our house's catechu, his underlying message wasn't tough to decode. For he wanted to get hold of that. Therefore, to protect my family's reputation, I would secretly climb onto the roof, and I shouldn't say steal but loot one or two catechus. As we know, the kings looted whenever they felt an imminent need or even when they didn't, and those who used to steal were sent to prison or executed by impalement.

During the winters, the girls would bask in the pleasant sunlight as if it was a customary family tradition and would shoo off crows. I was the only young brother-in-law in the house— being in charge of guarding my sister-in-law's *aamsatta*. Apart from that, I was her comrade in various petty domestic chores. I would read *Bangadhipa Parajaya* to her. And often allotted the task of cracking open the betel nut with a tool known as Jaanti, thereby delivering that task with finesse. My sister-in-law would not accept that I had other talents as well. She would point at my flawed looks until I blamed my fortune for the same. Nevertheless, she would appreciate my talent for shredding the betel nuts, and I would carry out my job of cutting betels quickly. Since nobody appreciated this talent of mine, thereby made use of my finely skilled hands (grown out of cutting betels) in other household tasks.

A rustic taste would linger in the feminine work done on the terrace. These existed in the days when there was a pounding room in which *Narus* were made. The maidservants rolled out cotton wicks on their thighs, and invitations would pour in from the neighbor's house on the eighth day after a child took birth. Kids nowadays do not get to hear fairytales; instead, they just read from their own books. These days, pickles and chutneys must be bought from the New Market, contained in corked bottles, and sealed with wax. The *Chandimandap*, once a major artifact of our time, has ceased to exist. Our Gurumoshai ran his pathshala (school) there. Not only the boys from our house but also little children from all around the neighborhood would go there to receive their primary education by scribbling letters on palm leaves. I, too, must have received my lessons in scratching from there. However, I faintly remember the kind of child I was back then. Unfortunately, as the telescope cannot trace the farthest planet in the solar system; similarly, I am unable to magnify that childhood image of mine.

My earliest lessons acquired from books were the tales at Sandamarka Muni's pathshala and the avatar Narasimha tearing apart the belly of Hiranyakasipu. Probably, I had seen this Narashima scene on a lead plate engraved in the book, and I had read some shlokas of Chanakya.

My place for holidaying was the unfenced roof from early childhood until adulthood; I spent my days in ways I pleased. When my father, Debendranath Tagore was home, he stayed in his room on the second floor. Behind the attic, I would stand and observe him from afar. On the terrace, he would meditate before sunrise and sit like a white statue with folded hands on his lap. Sometimes he would be away for a while in the mountains. In his absence, frequenting the roof was similar to the joy of crossing the seven seas. My daily affair would be to sit on the verandah and through the railings, stare at people moving to and fro in the street. However, to go up on that roof was to run away from the surging habitation of people. When you go there, you would unknowingly leave a footprint on the city and let your heart wander off to a place where the hue of the sky gets fused with the last green of the earth. Countless houses of different shapes and sizes would be visible to the naked eye, and within their gaps thronged bushy trees.

During the noons, I secretly frequented the terrace, a time that always held a special place in my heart. It was like enjoying the relaxing night hours but in the daytime. This turned me into a hermit and made me renounce everything. I would slip my hand through the shutter and unlock the door to the bedroom. There was a sofa right in front of the door where I would sit all alone. The servants, who were in charge of taking care of me, dozed off after having a full course meal, stretching out their bodies, and would lie down on the mat.

The sun turned tinted in roseate, whereas the eagles took flight, crying loudly. The bangle sellers passed over our alley, calling out to buyers.

Such quiet afternoons are gone, and so have vanished the quietude of the peddler. His sudden cry would penetrate the house walls and reach the housewife, lying on the pillow with her head tilted to the side. The maid would bring in the bangle seller, who would squeeze the tender wrists of the housewife to help her wear those beautiful bangles. The age at which a woman became a wife was different from today. Girls in those days got married off early in their lives. There was no sense of liberation at all; they remained confined to second grade. Whereas that bangle seller might be wandering off pulling rickshaws in that alley. The terrace was like the deserts I had read in books, swaying in all directions. The hot air gushes across it, whirling up the cloud of dust while the blue sky grows pale.

I had witnessed an oasis on this desert-clad roof. Nowadays, the tap water does not reach the top floor. But previously, water reached the second floor. I discovered the concealed bathroom entryway, almost like a young Livingston of Bengal. Turning on the tap, the water splashed out on my body. Thereafter, I would wipe off my body with a bedsheet and relax.

Gradually, the leisure hours came to an end. The clock on the porch struck 4 pm. The sky frowned strangely on a Sunday evening. The coming Monday's shadow fell as it was approaching to gobble it down in its eclipse. Down on the porch, the guards had started searching for the boy who managed to slip from their grip since it was snack time. This part of the day was like a red signal for Brajeshwar. He was in charge of buying snacks. In those days, the shopkeepers did not make a profit of thirty to forty percent from the actual price of the Ghee. In smell and taste, snacks had not yet been poisoned. If one could lay their hands on *Kochuri, Singara,* and *Alur Dam,* it wouldn't take long to gobble them down. But, just in time, when Brajeshwar would surface with his quintessential crooked neck and cry out, "Look, babu, what have I got for you!"

We would often find him with groundnuts in a cone-shaped packet. It's not that we were not interested in the groundnuts, but more so we were interested in his frugality. I never fussed about anything, not even when the *goja* popped out of the palm leaf wrapper.

As the daylight darkened, I saw the roof for the last time with a heavy heart. I looked down to find the geese climbing out of the pond. People have started pouring in at the ghat. The banyan tree extended its shadow across half the pond, whereas the clamors of the carriage bearers filled the street.

**Notes:**
Narad: In Hindu traditions, Narad Muni is a sage divinity who is well-known for being a traveling musician and storyteller.
*Riju Path*: A sanskrit reader by Vidyasagar.
*Bangadhipa Parajaya*: A book in two volumes by Pratapchandra Ghosh.
Aamsatta: Made of mango pulp mixed with sugar.
Chandimandap: A kind of canopy with an open side made for worshiping Durga.
Kochuri: Deep fried, puffy bread popular in Bengal.
Singara: Also known as samosa. Deep fried and stuffed with potatoes, peas and onions.
Alur Dom: Potato curry, popular in Bengal.

Days passed by in this dreary style. The school would scoop out an enormous part of the day, leaving the extra hours to remain dispersed over the morning and evening. As soon as I entered the class, the benches and tables would take a jab at my mind with their skinny elbows. They always looked this stiff. I would return home by the evening. The oil lamp in the study room summoned me like a signal to prepare the lessons for the next day.

Sometimes the master with his dancing bear would drop by our residence. Alongside the snake charmer, and some days a juggler would drop by. However, on Chitpur road, one can no longer hear the sound of the *dugdugi*. They have fled after saluting the cinema from afar as the latter has replaced such forms of entertainment.

My heart had also become pale like the dry days, similar to how the grasshopper stands on the withered leaves.

Suddenly, this monotony broke apart with the sound of a sanai. A new bride came home. She wore gold bracelets in her delicate brown hands. In the blink of an eye, the fences thrust open to welcome a woman from some distant magical land. I would wander far and wide but didn't dare to go near the new bride. She was exalted, being at the center of affection, while I was a playful child, nothing else.

Back then, the house was divided into two quarters known as mahals. Men would remain on the outside, whereas women would be on the inside. The royal behavior was still in practice. I remember my sister walking on the roof with the new wife and exchanging intimacies nonchalantly. As I attempted to draw close, I was pulled back with a rebuking tone, for this area was prohibited for boys. I thought with a dry face that it was time to return to my former days.

Not many games were accessible to us in those days. There were marbles and bat-ball (a distant cousin to cricket). And swung sticks or flew kites. The boys' games in the town were very ordinary. With all its running and jumping, football appeared far beyond our lives. Thereby, days I spent functioned like withered lifeless twigs of the same size, kept fencing me from all sides in a monotony.

And then, the rains descended from the distant mountains, which eroded the ancient banks in a moment. The same occurred even this year. The new wife introduced a new rule in the house. As her room adjoined the roof of the inner chamber, she had full control of the terrace.

It was the place where the leaf plates would be arranged for the dolls' weddings. On such a day, I would become the guest of honor. The new mistress could cook well and loved feeding too, and I readily satisfied the latter part of her hobby. When I returned home from school, my sister-in-law would be ready with the delicacies she had prepared herself. Somedays, she would serve me shrimp curry with soaked rice from yesterday, which would fill my heart with joy. Sometimes when she would go to the relative's house unable to find her slippers outside, I would hide something valuable from her room and set the course for an ensuing quarrel. I would interrogate, "Who will look after your room while you are away? Am I your watchman?" She would reply angrily, "You don't have to look after my room. Take care of yourself. That's enough."

Modern women will laugh at this childlike behavior. They might end up saying isn't there any other brother-in-law elsewhere who doesn't behave like this? I agree. Nowadays, people are more mature than they used to be. Those days, be they old or young, were joyous like a child.

And thereafter began another chapter on my lonely existence on the roof, and human company and friendship came. My brother, Jyotidada, would be the one who'd lit up these meetings.

**Notes:**

Dugdugi: It is an instrument that is a sort of two-headed drum being the instrument of Lord Shiva. Back in archaic days in Calcutta, hawkers would play this instrument while calling.

Jyotidada: Jyotirindranath Tagore

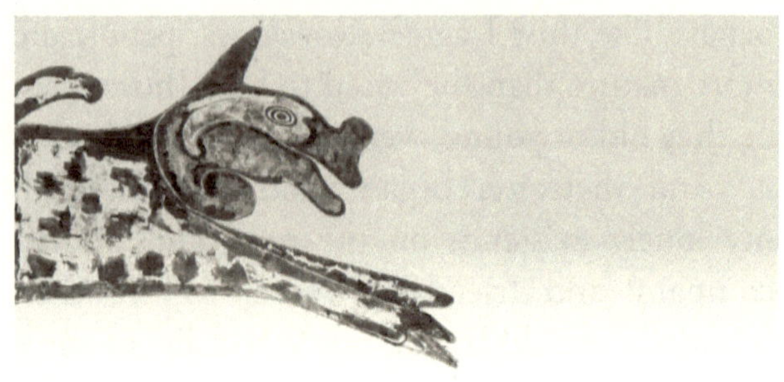

# 10

Fresh air embraced the roof kingdom and thus came a new season. At that time, my father left our Jorasanko house, and as he left, my brother Jyotidada came to stay with us. He placed himself in a room on the second floor, and seeing it as an opportunity that would benefit me, I reserved a little corner of his space for myself.

The curtain between the Andarmahal and Bahirmahal was finally dissolved. However, previously it was a big deal. During my childhood days, my Mejadada returned from England as a civilian. When he had to travel to Bombay for a job, he surprised everyone outside the family by taking his wife along with him. He felt it unethical to leave his wife behind. So, he took her to a foreign land and never attempted to hide this fact. It was a rebellious act. The family was in shock.

While going out, appropriate outfits for the girls were not yet in trend. My sister-in-law was the first person to start this fashion of wearing sarees, which has now become an everyday thing. Earlier, the little girls had not yet begun wearing frocks or swinging their braided hair—at least, not in our family. The little ones behaved like people from Peshawar as they wore pathani suits. When Bethune school was inaugurated, my elder sister was very young then, and she was the pioneer who made the road easy for girls who wanted a formal education. She was very fair and didn't seem like an Indian girl. I once heard how my sister got held up by the police while going to school in a palanquin. The police officers mistook her for an abducted English girl because of her outfit.

I have already said there was no communication bridge between the young and the old. However, amid such archaic rules, Jyotidada came with a fresh mind. I was almost twelve years younger than him. Despite a massive age gap, he would still notice me, which was surprising. What was more surprising was that he didn't ever stop me from speaking or complaining about having a big mouth. I was very fortunate, for I was not discouraged from thinking aloud. Today, I live among all kinds of boys. I can at least go on talking about five subjects or so. However, they always keep mum. God knows what prevents them from asking questions. I understand that these are children from old age where the elders were supposed to talk while the young were instructed to stay silent. The children of today's age have the courage to ask questions unlike the ones back then, who accepted everything by hanging their heads low.

A piano was brought to the room, which was attached to the roof. Then came the modern burnished furniture from Bowbazar. My heart swelled up in pride on seeing these. It was almost as if before my poor eyes appeared the cheap abundance of modern times.

After that, my fountain of music was set loose, and Jyotidada would compose new melodies on the piano while he kept me by his side. My job was to take note of all the compositions and supply words to the tunes that Jyotidada made then and there.

At the end of the day, mats and pillows would be organized on the terrace. There would remain a thick garland of Bel flowers on a silver plate wrapped in damp handkerchiefs, ice-cold water in a saucepan, and a bowl full of *paan*.

After taking a bath and tying her hair, my sister-in-law would be ready to sit with us. Jyotidada, clad in a shawl, would start playing the violin. Following the scale, I would sing a high-pitched song. Until then, God had not yet taken back the tonal quality He had endowed me with. Under the sunset sky, my music would sway across roofs. The south wind came with a gentle puff from the distant sea, and the stars filled the sky.

My sister-in-law had converted the entire roof into a garden and nothing less. She had arranged rows of long palm trees in casks around them, where bloomed Chameli, Gandharaj, Rajanigandha, Karabi, and Dolonchapa. Of course, the idea that the roof might get damaged didn't cross her mind, but everyone was attentive in this case.

Akshay Chowdhury would come in very often. He knew he was out of tune. Others knew more about this characteristic of his. However, his stubbornness to sing didn't get subdued in any case. He especially loved the Behag Raga and sang with his eyes shut. Therefore, he couldn't notice the listeners' expressions. He took whatever he deemed fit that would resonate. Transformed it into his left tabla and would beat it in blissful assimilation while nibbling his lips in his sincerity. If he found a hardcover book, then that, too, would equally satisfy his purpose. He was a kind of idealist and therefore didn't make any difference between his holidays and working days.

The evening concert would gradually come

to an end. I had always been a nocturnal boy who would sleep in the mornings. During the nighttime, I would roam as a minion of *Brahmadatyi* while the entire neighborhood went to bed. On a moonlit night, the shadows of the rows of trees on the roof fell on the floor, creating patterns like a dreamscape *Alpona*. Outside the roof, the young tree would sway-tumble in the breeze while the leaves shimmered in harmony. But something caught my attention; the small attic with a sloping roof across the lane. It looked as if it was pointing toward something.

As the clock stroke, 1 at night or 2 am. A howling chant arises from the street—*Bolo Hari, Hari bol!*

**Notes:**
Hori Bol: Popularly known as the chant that is made in funerals of the Hindus in Bengal.
Mejadada: Satyendranath Tagore
Alpana: Patterns painted on the floor in times of auspicious occasions in Bengal.

# 11

Earlier, it was a trend in every household to keep caged birds. I would always get irritated to hear the Koel cry from a neighborhood house. My sister-in-law had brought in a Shyama bird from China. It whistled a fountain of tune from under a cloth that shrouded its cage. Besides this, there were birds of other breeds, and their cages were strung up in the west corner of the verandah. Every morning an insect hawker would provide the bird with food. He had grasshoppers and grain flour for birds that fed on grains.

Jyotidada would always have an answer to all my arguments, which I couldn't expect from women in general. For example, once my sister-in-law wanted to keep squirrels in a cage. I strongly protested and told her that it was wrong to do so. She told me that there was no need for me to pretend like her teacher, which was, of course, as you can see, not the right way to answer. Therefore, instead of going into an argument, I secretly snuck two creatures and set them free. After that, I was rebuked but didn't pay any attention. However, there was a fixed topic on which my sister-in-law and I would quarrel that never came to an end. Let me tell you about that topic:

There was a clever man called Umesh, who brought in scraps of silk of varied colors from English tailoring shops at a very cheap rate. He made garments for women with it by adding cheap laces and a bit of net. Umesh would open his packet and spread them before the women of the house. He would claim the clothes in fashion. He spelled it like some mantra that the ladies couldn't avoid. I can't say how troubled I was upon hearing that. Repeatedly I objected after feeling more and more restless. In return, I have been hurled with a reply—don't behave like an uncle; act your age. I told my sister-in-law that the black-bordered, classic Dhakai sarees were better than these. I wonder, nowadays, don't the modern brothers-in-law have a say when they find their sisters-in-law in georgette sarees like painted dolls? Though Umesh's sewn works were not as bad as those were. Back then, women didn't carry any forgery on their faces.

I have always lost to my sister-in-law in every

single argument since she would not provide any clear answer to any of my questions. Also, I kept losing in chess as she was an expert.

Since Jyotidada's name came up, there are a few things that need to be told for the readers to have a clear understanding of him. To do that, I would have to look back.

Jyotidada traveled to Shilaidaha quite often to look after his zamindari business. Once, he took me along with him, for which people frowned since they thought it to be an unconventional thing. He definitely must have thought that this idea of traveling away from home would be an important lesson. He was aware of my mind, how it wandered off to the azuring winds and open air, from which I drew my hunger. Shortly after that, when I got promoted in the school of life, it was in Shilaidaha where I kept aging with time.

The old indigo factory stood unimpaired. The river *Padma* was far from there. The zamindar's office was on the ground floor, whereas our living quarters were on the upper story. It had a colossal sundeck up in the front. Outside stood large palm trees that had grown over time alongside Mr. Nilkar's progressing business. Today, the thundering howls of Sahibs have fallen silent. Where has the indigo factory's hellish messenger vanished to? Where have all the troops of constables with staves disappeared to? Where has the vast dining room with all the tables, where the gentlemen would come on horseback, meet and converse from day until night, disappeared to? Alongside the feast, people would dance in pairs. While the intoxication of champagne bubbled in their blood! The lamentable cries of the ryots didn't reach their bosses' ears, whose power extended to the district jail.

All such traces of those times have vanished into thin air. The facts that have survived from the past are the graves of two sahibs. While the tall palm trees would sway in the breeze, the grandchildren of the peasants of that day would now and again witness the ghost of the Sahibs—wandering in the creepy garden of the house.

I decided to stay alone in my little corner room; the vast open terrace took up the entirety of my leisure time. My leisure days were sanctioned from a distant land, obscure as dark waters of some ancient lake. The *Bou-Katha-Kao* called ceaselessly, and thoughts popped into my mind. With these thoughts, my notebook had begun to fill up with verses, like the blossoms from a mango tree when it first blooms in the month of *Magh*.

In those days, if a young boy or a girl who diligently, after counting syllables, could pen down two lines of verse, the wise people of this country would think that to be a result of some unique talent. There were female poets whom I had come across who had already appeared in print. The old-fashioned, which means the careful construction of poems by using fourteen letters and thereby creating rhyming and metrical patterns, have been replaced by works of modern girls.

Boys were far less courageous than girls and shyer as well. Nevertheless, I can't remember any other young boy to have penned down poetry other than me. One day, an elder nephew told me that if I could place the fourteen letters in some template, it'd become poetry. And indeed, I witnessed this magic as it came true from my hands—the lotus of poetry bloomed from the mold of fourteen syllables, and even the bumblebee sat on it. My differences with the poets disappeared in no time, and my attempt has been the same since then.

I remember when I was in the junior class of our high school, our superintendent Gobindababu, heard a rumor that I wrote poetry. He then asked me to write one; he thought it would bring glory to the school. So I had to write and recite it in front of the entire class, and when I did, I had to hear that it was plagiarized. Although critics had not been able to find that, later, when I grew wiser, I became highly skilled in stealing thoughts, not verse. However, stolen goods were precious things.

I recall once composing a poem to express my sorrow that combined the *Payar* and *Tripadi* meters. The feeling was akin to what I felt when my arms started making waves as I swam to pick a lotus blossom. The more I drew myself closer to it, the further it floated off by the rippling waves. Akshay babu took me to his relative's house and made me recite the poem. They remarked, "The boy has a gift for writing verses."

Whereas Bouthakuron's (my sister-in-law) behavior was just the opposite. She didn't have faith that I might become a writer someday. She'd tell me that I would never be able to write like Biharilal Chakraborty. Then, I would sulk and think, had my writing matched the standard of someone lower than Mr. Chakraborty, it would also prevent her from insulting her little brother-in-law's disapproval of female fashion.

Jyotidada loved riding horses. He would take Bouthakuron on a ride from Chitpur Road to Eden Gardens. He gave me a pony in Shilaidaha, which was by no means a runner. He sent me on it to make it run on the Rathatola ground. So somehow, I managed to maintain my balance as I made it run on that rugged ground. Jyotidada believed that I would not fall, and I didn't, maybe because the pony was determined not to let me do so. A few years later, Jyotidada even made me run on horseback across the streets in Kolkata. It wasn't a pony but a mature and moody horse.

One day it took me on its back and ran straight from the porch to the yard, where it received its grain feed. From that day on, I parted ways with him.

I had already mentioned how Jyotidada was skilled in using the gun. He has always had the desire to hunt down tigers. One day Biswanath, the hunter, told him that a tiger was lurking in the forest in Shilaidaha. Then he readied himself with his gun, and strangely he took me along. Due to his decision, the thought of some crisis that must arise didn't occur to him. Biswanath was an expert and knew there was nothing manly in shooting from the *macha*. He'd call the tiger out and shoot it from the front, and he has never missed a target.

The jungle is dense, and the tiger refuses to show itself in its shadows. A ladder was made out by cutting footholds in bamboo, on which Jyotidada made his way up to the top with a rifle. I wasn't wearing shoes and didn't even have the option to kick the tiger if it chased me. Biswanath gave us a signal while Jyotidada tried hard to see it, and finally, a tiger stripe appeared in his naked eye after a while. He shot the tiger immediately, and down it went as the bullet had struck the tiger's spine. It failed to stand up and bit every twig and branch it found within its reach; growling and swishing its tail, the tiger grew restless. When you think about it, it's strange that the tiger waited patiently to die, which is not in their fierce nature. I wonder whether it was fed opium before its dinner the night before. Why was it so sleepy?

There was another time when a tiger came to the jungles of Shilaidaha. My brother and I set out on an elephant in search of him. The elephant went majestically as it uprooted the sugarcane field and munched as it moved forward, it was as if we were in the middle of an earthquake. Thus appeared the forest before us. The elephant crushed the trees with its feet, pulled them with his trunk, and flung them to the ground. Earlier, I had heard something from Biswanath's brother Chamru: it gets dangerous when the tiger jumps up the elephant's back and pierces its claws. Then the elephant starts running in pain through the forest, and people lodged on its back get smashed against the trees or branches—eventually, no sign is left of them.

That day, when I was sitting on its back, the thoughts of getting my bones and head smashed were clouding my mind. I kept this fear of mine to be a complete secret. Showing a daredevil attitude, I looked here and there as if I would take care of the situation if I caught a glimpse of the tiger. The elephant rushed into the forest and then walked to a place and fell completely still. The *Mahout* didn't even urge the elephant to move forward, for he had more faith in the

tiger from amongst the two hunters (one being my brother). He was concerned that Jyotidada might wound the tiger so badly that the latter would become desperate. Suddenly the tiger leaped out of a bush akin to a thunderbolt it came tearing up the clouds. We were used to seeing cats, dogs, and jackals, and here, this was such a powerful creature, gallant and beautiful. The elephant ran through the open field in the midday sun. How lovely it moved at such speed! This was the perfect time to watch the tiger in the open ground in the glare of the sunlight.

There is one more thing, which might appear funny, which concerns a gardener in Shilaidaha who plucked flowers and arranged them in vases. A thought ran across my mind that the vibrant sap of flowers might serve as inspiration for my verse. However, the moisture I found by squeezing the flowers hardly came to the pen nib. I decided to create a machine for that purpose. If I made a wooden bowl with a hole in the middle and a grinder around it, the purpose would be served. It could be turned on a wheel tied to a rope. Therefore, I took the case to Jyotidada. Maybe he smiled deep inside but didn't show any sign outside. Accordingly, he ordered, and thus came the carpenter with all the woods and his instruments and created the machine. Filling the bowl with flowers, I tried moving the grinder attached to the rope continually, and the more I tried, the more the flowers got crushed to a muddy paste instead of rendering the juice. Jyotidada noticed that the flower juice and grinding machine were useless, yet he did not laugh at my face.

This was only once when I got down to show my engineering skills. There is a saying in the Hindu scriptures that when a person presumes to become something that he isn't, a god appears to humiliate that person. Similarly, on that day, a god had looked down on me mockingly as I tried to be an engineer; since then, I have stopped putting my hands on machines. I had not even dared to tune the Esraj.

I have described in *Jiban Smriti* how Jyotidada went bankrupt while trying to compete with the Flotilla company by running a Swadeshi streamer company in the rivers in Bangladesh. Bouthakuron had passed away long before that. After a while, Jyotidada left his room on the second floor and went away. He ended up on a hilltop in Ranchi, where he built himself a house.

**Notes:**
Biharilal Chakraborty: A Bengali poet and music composer.
Payar: Bengali verse in syllables amounting to 14.
Tripadi: Metric style in Bengali.
Macha: A heightened platform.
Dhakai: Bearing the name from the capital city of Bangladesh, Dhakai sarees are made with cotton.

Bou Katha Kao: Indian cuckoo.
Mahout: Indian elephant rider.
Bouthakuron: Kadambari Debi, wife of Jyotirindranath Tagore.
Magh: Held to be the tenth month in the Bengali calendar.

# 12

After that, a new act that altered my life began amid the drama of the second-floor room. I had lived like a gypsy throughout, starting one day in a palanquin and one day in the granary. I would be sometimes here and sometimes there. When Bouthakuron came, a garden appeared on the roof, a piano got installed, and fountains of melodies shimmered.

The shade of the attic on the eastern side would be the place for Jyotidada to drink his coffee. He would then read the first draft of his new play. He'd sometimes summon me to help him with my unpractised hands—to add a few verses. Gradually, the sunshine would advance, and from above the shade, we would hear the crows cry, up on the roof, as they looked down on a piece of bread. Finally, at 10 am, the shade dissipated, and the terrace became scorching hot.

At noon, Jyotidada would leave for his office on the ground floor. Bouthakuron would peel off the fruits, cut and arrange them on silver plates. Those plates would also have a few sweetmeats made by her, garnished with rose petals. There would also be glasses containing coconut water, fruit juice, or Palmyra palm kernels cooled in ice. Covering them with an embroidered silk handkerchief, they were placed on a Morabadi tray and would be taken to the ground floor office at about one or two o'clock in noon.

*Bangadarshan* was quite famous back then. Characters created by Bankim Chandra Chattopadhyay garnered popularity when *Suryamukhi* and *Kundanandini* started going from one house to the other as if being one of their own. People were able to relate to that. What would happen to them was of great concern to people all around the country. Whenever *Bangadarshan* arrived in our neighborhood, people didn't care to take an afternoon nap. It happened to my advantage that I didn't have to snatch it from anyone because I had the talent of being a charming reader. Instead of reading on her own, Bouthakuron would love to hear me read it aloud before her. At that time, there was no electric fan. So I would acquire a part of relaxation rendered by the hand fan as she waved it before my face while I read the text.

**Notes:**
Morabadi: A place in Ranchi
*Bangadarshan*: A magazine edited by Bankim Chandra Chatterjee
Suryamukhi and Kundanandini: Characters in Bishabriksha by Bankim

# 13

Jyotidada would sometimes be out in the garden on the banks of the Ganges—for a change of air. The Ganges had not yet lost its purity with the dwellings embarked upon by the ensuing foreign business. The bird's nests on either side didn't set adrift. The iron machines, which had chimneys that resembled elephant trunks, had not released their black toxic gas into the clean air.

The first house I can think of standing beside the Ganges had two stories. As it began raining, cloud-clad shadows floated along the wavy skies. The shadows continue to darken and condense at the top of the opposite forest shore. I have often composed my songs on such days. But, that day was different from the usual ones. The words of Vidyapati lurked in my mind:

*E bhara Badara, Mah Badara*
*Sunya Mandir More*
[Overflowed with a downpour in the period of
Bhadra—
August-September—
Empties my soul's home stands]

I made its melody with a tinge of a Raga and
called it my own. The memory of that rainy day
on the Ganges shore still lurks in the caskets of
my rain songs. I remember the winds flurrying
against the branches on the tree top; while
boughs and branches getting tangled up, the
dinghy boats raising their white sails continued
to battle against the wind. The waves break
against the shore with sharp smacking sounds.
When Bouthakuron came back, I sang my song
to her. She didn't give her feedback but listened
very quietly. I was about 16 or 17 then, but still,
we argued over foolish things, though the spirit
of it had lessened due to the passing of time.

There were a variety of colored glasses
on the windows of our rooms, which were of
different heights. Floors were made of marble,
and a sprawling verandah seemingly appeared
suspended above the Ganges. There I would
stay awake at night and would try to match
the rhythm of strolling, as I usually did, with
what I would do later in my life on the banks
of Sabarmati. But, unfortunately, the garden has

ceased to exist with the automation of the Dandi factory.

At times, I would remember how occasionally feasting took place under the Bakul tree in Moran Sahib's garden. It didn't have a lot of spices, but the cooking showed skillful mastery. For example, when my brother and I had our Paite, Bouthakuron would cook *Havishyanne* for us, which had a topping with pure ghee. Over three days, its taste and its smell lured everyone.

I didn't fall sick easily, which was my biggest problem. At the same time, the rest of the boys who managed to fall sick received Bouthakuron's care. Not only did they receive care, but they also consumed the maximum time of her schedule, and my share would consequently get reduced. So that day, the chapter with the third story hence ended with Bouthakuron's untimely death. After that, the second floor became mine; however, it could not be compared with the older days. Oops! I must apologize for having wandered to the steps of manhood. I must at once return to my boyhood in my narrative— this time I have to give an account of my doings when I was sixteen. Before I stepped on to this age, *Bharati* had already been published.

Nowadays, people are very excited to publish magazines all over the country. I can sometimes understand such driving enthusiasm when I look back at the madness of that age. A boy like me who had no knowledge and could not afford it found himself a place in the meetings—to which nobody noticed—concerning the magazine. This explains how the trend of young ones stepping in everywhere was rising. The only established journal then was titled *Bangadarshan*. But, unfortunately, our *Bharati* failed to reach its standards. What my elder brother wrote was hard to understand in terms of handwriting, and we also faced difficulty decoding its meaning. And, in the middle of all these, I ended up writing a story, the crude verbosity of whose style I was too youthful to even think about assessing, nor did others possess the critical judgment to do so.

Now is the time to tell you about my Borodada. Jyotidada lived on the third floor, whereas my Borodada stayed in a room on the southern verandah. At one phase, he was immersed in heavy theories bubbling in his mind, far beyond our reach. Many people listened to what he wrote or thought; if somebody agreed to provide company, Borodada wouldn't let that person leave quickly, and likewise; it was solely not because of the urge of the latter to listen to his philosophies but something beyond that. There was a fellow whose name I cannot remember, but everyone called him 'Philosopher.' The rest of my brothers mocked him simply not for his craving for the mutton chop but his urgent necessities. Apart from philosophy, Borodada loved making mathematical equations. The southern verandah was scattered with papers containing mathematical signs and symbols. He couldn't sing but could play a foreign flute, which was not to accompany any song. Instead, he used it to measure the notes of each scale mathematically.

After that he started writing *Swapna-Prayana*. Firstly, he began making a verse measuring the sound values of the Sanskrit words and thereby weighed them in the scales of Bengali rhythm in a format. He kept some and discarded some— torn pages remained scattered everywhere. After that, he would write poetry; the amount he wrote was much less than the amount of poetry he threw away. He didn't like the things he penned pretty quickly. We were not wise enough to pick up his discarded rhymes. Whatever he wrote, he would read out to us, and people would gather around him. The sweetness of his poetry enthralled everyone in the household. We would burst laughing in the middle of our studies. He would laugh generously at the skies, and if someone chanced to be beside him, that person would get slapped because of Borodada's hurling hands and legs while he laughed hysterically. The Jorasanko house had a fountain of life which was this southern verandah. But the fountain dried up as my Borodada left for Santiniketan and settled there in the ashram.

I sometimes recall how wonderful that garden was opposite our southern verandah and whenever the autumnal sunbeam of the Sharat dispersed across the garden, I would compose and sing a new song:

*Today the autumn sun, the dawning dreams*
*Whiffs a yearning I know not in my heart*

Alongside this, I also remember to have composed one song in blazing noon—

*Eluding all the while*
*What is thy game in my heart*

Borodada had another openly noticeable talent and that was swimming. Whenever he got down in the pond, he would swim at least fifty laps before coming out. During his stay at the *Peneti garden*, he would swim far out into the Ganges. Getting inspired by him, we, too, learned how to swim on our own. We stretched our wet pajamas to fill them with air. No matter how hard we tried, it swelled out around our waist like an air belt, and it wouldn't let us drown. When I grew old and resided in Shilaidaha, I once swam across the *Padma*. No matter how impressive it might sound, it wasn't a fanciful one. At times there wasn't any current on the *Padma* that one might fear, even though I had already used

the stories to impress others quite a few times. When I went to Dalhousie as a child, my father never forbade me to wander alone. I would go from one hill to the other with a walking stick. It appeared amusing to scare myself because of my make-believe situation. Once while walking down a hill, I stepped on a heap of leaves at the foot of a tree. As I was about to stumble down, I somehow balanced myself with the stick. However, I might have needed help to stop myself. I wondered how long it would take me to roll down the slope to the waterfall. I told my mother what could've happened, and I told her how strolling amidst the pine forest, I might change a situation to fall in front of a bear. Well, I couldn't refrain from the joy of talking about it. Since nothing happened, I stacked all of these unfortunate events up in my imagination. The story of me crossing the river *Padma* isn't much different from these stories.

When I was seventeen, I stepped down from the editorial board of *Bharati*. At this time, the decision had been made for me to go to England. Furthermore, it was decided that before sailing abroad, I should learn all the essential English manners from my Mejdada. He was a judge then in Ahmedabad, and his wife and his kids are in England. They were waiting for Mejdada to get a furlough and join them. So I was uprooted from one field and brought to the other. I was made to get accustomed to a new environment. From the beginning, only shyness crept in, and the thought of introducing myself to new people and how I would protect my image before them bothered me. It was not easy to be just an acquaintance in an unfamiliar world, and I didn't have a choice but to avoid them. Therefore, a boy like me would stumble along the way. In Ahmedabad, my mind wandered off to an old historical image. The Judge used to live in Shahibag, the former palace of the Mughals. My brother would leave for work at noon. The big house would then be all empty, and I would loiter around like a possessed one. There was a terrace and a large paved platform. From there, I could easily see the river Sabarmati whose water level would reach the knee level while zigzagging through the sands. I felt like the stone-built tanks, dispersed by and large on the deck, carried the stories of the Begums and their wealthy bathing halls.

We grew up in Calcutta, where we had no exposure to historical grandeur. Our vision had narrowed down due to the boundaries. In Ahmedabad only, I got the chance to witness that history. Since the place subsumed in history had frozen, I got a chance to glance back at the aristocratic past. The former days appeared like Yaksha treasures buried deep inside the ground. From there, I got the first suggestion for incorporating into my story Hungry Stones.

Well, that appears like an age-old story. But, then, in the *nahabat khana* (Drum House), an orchestra played day and night, horses' hooves echoed through the streets, the cavalry of the Turkish army continued their march past, and sunlight shimmered upon their spears. In the royal court, all kinds of dangerous whispers were going on. Negro eunuchs stood outside the Andarmahal with open swords guarding it. Rose water fountain ran in Begum's hammams, and the tinkering sounds of bangles filled the air. But today, Shahibag stood still and almost appeared to have fallen silent like a forgotten tale, colorless, devoid of sounds—days remained dry, and nights bereft of taste.

Ancient history seems to lie there with its bare skeleton. Just the skull remains, no crown. I have covered the head with an outer cover and have been able to position the statue in the magical chambers of my mind. The way I created a background against which it stood was also a byproduct of my imagination. Some can be remembered, and because I forget most things, managing like this is more accessible. After eighty years, even my picture doesn't correspond line by line with reality; much of it has been made up.

After staying here for some time, Mejdada decided that he would introduce me to girls who would make me feel at home in England. That was also the best way for me to learn the English language. So for a few days, I stayed with a family in Bombay where one of its residents was a girl who had just returned from England after completing her education. I could have been more knowledgeable. Therefore, if she ignored me, it would not be her fault. However, she did not do such a thing, lacking any bookish knowledge to offer her, I was waiting for a chance to tell her that I had the skill of writing poetry. This was my only asset to impress her, and as soon as I told her this, she didn't take this lightly but rather was impressed by it. She asked, "Can you give me a nickname, dear poet?" I replied, "Well, certainly," and gave her a name that suited her perfectly. I wanted to use that name and entwin it with my verse. So I placed it in the structure of a poem and sang it to her in the morning Bhairavi raga. After listening to it, she told me, "O poet, your song can make me come to life even from my deathbed."

From this, one will clearly understand that while admiringly appreciating someone, girls add a bit of honey and exaggerate it to the person they want to caress. I can remember she was the first person to have appreciated my face. The praise was, of course, very delicately imparted. For example, once she told me, "You have to keep my word; never grow a beard. You should never mask your facial profile."

I had not been able to keep her word to this date, for everyone knows about this. But, unfortunately, she passed away long before even disobedience manifested on my face.

A few years later, birds from some foreign land would come and build nests on our Banyan tree. Then, they would fly away long before I understood how their wings danced. They would bring unknown tunes from a distant land. Similarly, some angels from a small and unexpected house would cross our path in our life journey, widening the boundaries of our hearts' content. They would appear without us calling, and one day, calling them would not bring them back. However, as they left, they dropped a piece of floral patchwork on the life sheet. Forever and ever, the price of day and night exalts us.

**Notes:**

Paite: Also known as upanayana which is a sacred thread ceremony in Brahmanic tradition marking the spiritual rebirth of the child.

Havishyanne: is the unadulterated and simple to-process food given by yogis when they do their 'sadhana' or compensation while seeking god or truth.

*Swapna Prayana*: A book in verse by Dwijendranath Tagore

Borodada: Dwijendranath Tagore

Mejdada: Satyendranath Tagore

*Bharati*: a monthly magazine founded by Jyotirindranath

Tagore and edited by his eldest brother Dwinjendranath Tagore.
Peneti Garden: An estate where the Tagore family frequented, which belonged to Asutosh Deb

# 14

The creator who had been instrumental in making me made his first model on Bengali soil. I would describe this model as my childhood. There aren't many elements in it. Although only a few ingredients were ingrained in me—some of them came from my family's hard work—others from the atmosphere of my home. Quite often, the mold work comes to a standstill at this stage. In addition, some people are shaped by the education factory, which eventually turns out to be suitable products for the market devoid of any organic conditioning.

Fortunately, I had the opportunity to avoid anything in the factory. The pundits who were in charge of educating me soon gave up. Even Gyanchandra Bhattacharya (BA), the son of Anandachandra Vedantabagish, realized that I could never be driven on the road of learning. Wise men of that era were not convinced that boys should be cast in the mold of learned graduates. Back then, there was no demand for the rich and poor to be led to the same college for further studies. Our family had no wealth but a name, so the tradition strived. They were also indifferent toward a traditional college education.

Hailing from lower financial strata, I received a scholarship to move into De Cruz's Bengal Academy. My parents had hoped that my fluency in English would be tutored. However, I was almost deaf and dumb in the Latin class while all my textbooks remained plain, empty, and pure like a widow's cloth. Witnessing my insistence on not studying, my class teacher complained about this to Mr. De Cruz. In response, De Cruz said that we were not born in this world to explore but pay our monthly fees. Even Gyanbabu had no option but to accept it, he smartly carved a way to please his terms. First, he made me learn *Kumarasambhava* by heart. Then locking me up at home, he made me translate Macbeth into Bengali. On the other hand, Pundit Ramsarvasa taught me *Shakuntala*. He set me free from the fixed curriculum and got some reward as a resultant action. This was my way out to find the ingredients that sparked my imagination, and there were loads of Bengali books. I made no discrimination in whatsoever books I picked randomly.

As soon as I went to London, my life began with a series of craftsmanship; the result is what in chemistry is called a compound. The only thing of fortune was that I acquired knowledge by learning traditionally—I managed some but not completely. Mejobouthan and her children were there, but my mind was longing for my homeland. I traversed around my school, and a teacher taught me, and I also ignored that. However, there were a few things that I acquired. They allowed me to stay in touch with people. The atmosphere of England started to take over my mind. Mr. Palit freed me from the confinement of the house. I moved into a doctor's home where he and his family made me forget I was in a foreign land, away from home. Mrs. Scott showered her genuine affection on me. She always cared for me like my mother. I was then admitted to the University of London. Henry Morley taught English Literature at that time. His teachings were not as barren as one would extract from dead books. Literature completely kindled life in his brain also, in his voice, it came to our inward creatures where the spirit looks for its sustenance, and nothing of its fundamental nature was lost. As soon as I returned home, I would read books by the Clarendon Press. In other words, I had the task of mastering myself.

At times Mrs. Scott would feel that my face was pale, and she became restless. She didn't realize that I hardly got sick in my growing years. She didn't know I regularly bathed in ice-cold water. The doctors found my action unjust.

I studied at the university for three months. However, I learned primarily from people I knew personally back home. Our artisan, seizing the opportunity, added ingredients to the creator's composition. I shared a tender intimacy with English hearts for three months, resulting from the fusion of varied elements. I had to read verse-drama, and history to others every evening until 11 pm. I learned a lot in a short period. It was not curriculum-based learning, but I got close to human hearts and minds.

Though I went to England, I did not become a barrister. I didn't earn substantial experience to stir the foundational value of my life. In my heart, I united the East with the West, instead. It rendered me with a vision to realize the significance of my name *Robi*.

**Notes:**
*Kumarasambhava* is an Epic written by Kalidasa.
Mejobouthan: Gyanandanandini Debi, wife of
Satyendranath Tagore
Robi: It means Sun, it is used in this context because the same doesn't distinguish between the East and West.

## THE LAD

Age, then, was fresh and light
Like a wingless bird, couldn't take a flight
Flap flap, on the neighboring roof, up pigeon -flocks go
A crow on our balcony rail, let its cawing flow
From the lane across, the hawker cry
With *Topshe* in *gamcha*-clad basket, asks all to try
On the roof, sat my dada with his violin soon
To the evening star, he would pick it up and tune

Leaving my English lesson, to Boudidi I would flee
Covered she her face with a red-bordered saree
I hid the stolen keys, in the flowerpot
Her temper and love for me, I would sought
Kishori Chatterjee would arrive with the evening call
On his left hand a hookah and right shoulder hung a shawl

Fast he went reading Labkush rhyme
Lied my copy open, without any dime
In my heart wish played it's charm
If *Panchali* team took me in its arm
Studies stalled thoughts of mine to clutter
How I wished to sing songs in different countries and flutter

Quickly after school reaching close to my home
Whitey clouds landed on roof to roam
Down the rain comes, floods the road
Like *Airavat's* trunk, the pipes overflowed
In darkness pitter patter little bit of rain
Prince on the road, is lost like swain.
Rivers and hills on the map hung
Kunlun, and Mississippi and young Si Kiang
Knew what I all were heard from afar
In many colors, weaved nets posed like a star
Goes around different sounds dangling and dancing
With an airy world, my mind gleefully ring
Thoughts in bundles, whirl, and twirl
Like moss on river, under clouds, birds unfurl

From *Picture of Rhymes*
Shantiniketan,
Asadha, 1344

**Notes:**
Airavat: Elephant, belonging to Indra as stated in Hindu scriptures.
Gamcha: A handmade towel popular in India.
Topse: A small fish popular in Bengal.

A self-portrait by Tagore

# About the Translator

**Somudranil Sarkar**, a theater artiste for over twenty-one years, is a postgraduate in English language and literature. He published *C/O Bonolata Sen*, a collection of short stories, in 2019. His work has appeared in *Strange Horizons*, *The Critical Flame*, and elsewhere. In addition, Sarkar often curates workshops on theater and pantomime. As a performer, he meddles between the esoteric and the unexplored itinerary.